The Frugal Home

By M. Kaye Hash
www.thefrugalhome.com

What kind of home do you live in? Is it full of love, good times, and happiness? If it is, are you wealthy? Chances are you aren't wealthy, as the majority of people in the world make under $100,000 a year, and many have incomes much less than that. Money is good for a great deal of things but it isn't great at buying the things that really matter. Living a frugal life is a great way to live a life of love, good times, and happiness whether you have a large amount of money to draw from or not.

What does frugal mean to you? For many, it's thought of as being cheap and never buying anything fun, or never taking a vacation, or not buying any of the new toys that your neighbors have. This isn't true. The frugal home doesn't necessarily mean the poor house or the misers down the road. You don't have to be poor to be frugal, nor do you have to live a miserable existence in order to be frugal.

Frugality is a way of looking at life. It is about the most economical use of all of your resources, not just the cash in your pockets. It is about using what you have if it is efficient and a good use of funds, not just using something because it is cheap. It is about quality over quantity. For instance, an old water heater may be costing you more on your electrical bill than what you could save if you bought a brand-new, efficient water heater. When you go shopping, you will probably not want to buy the cheapest water heater as it will most likely not be as efficient as a more expensive model. You do not want to save $100 at the point of purchase only to have the appliance cost you ten dollars more a month on your utility bill; in less than a year the cheaper one will have actually cost you more money. Just because something may look like the cheapest option doesn't make it the most frugal option or the most efficient use of your hard-earned cash.

Every aspect of our homes and lives can be looked at through a frugal lens, from your grocery bill to saving the environment. Look at living a frugal life whether you need to get out of debt or just want to reduce your consumption and improve your health.

While frugality is a lifestyle choice for many, you can take from it the parts that you will use if the whole doesn't appeal to you, or you may find that you are more frugal at certain times in your life more than others. You can take one step at a time into a frugal life, you do not have to jump in feet first and change everything about the way you live. Creating a frugal home for some is best done with slow changes that allow you to look at the resources you have in entirely new ways. Beginning to live a frugal life is much like beginning a new diet; you are much more likely to stick with it if you start with slow changes instead of trying to make many drastic changes that you will not stick to.

Frugality isn't a race. It's a journey through life.

My Frugal Journey

I didn't become frugal overnight. At first, I didn't even know that what I was doing would be considered frugal, I just wanted to get out of debt and didn't want to keep watching my money soar out quicker than it trickled in.

Years ago, my husband and I were in $11,000 worth of credit card debt. Not mortgage debt, not car debt, not even school loan debt. We were $11,000 in credit card debt alone on top of any other debt. We were barely in our mid-twenties. We had spent our early twenties "living it up", but we had grown up (some!) and had begun to have goals that exceeded past what bar we would attend that weekend. Our biggest goal was to own our own home but our credit score was 535. Essentially, we wouldn't have qualified for a sub-prime loan in an age where just about everyone was getting a loan. We knew we had to pay off our debt in order to fulfill our dreams.

It took us two years. Two years in which I learned a great deal about credit cards, debt, and frugal living in general, in order to pay off our debt. Instead of wasting all of our money we started putting any extra toward our debt. One year after our credit card debt was paid off we purchased our first home, a 900 square foot single wide on two and a half acres. The single wide was so old that it wasn't even considered a home; it was listed as a "fixture", much the same as our two bay garage and small barn. Essentially, on paper, we had just bought some land.

We had always lived off of one income; we never made a conscious decision to do that but having lived that way for so long made it much easier for me to decide I would try working from home instead of working outside of the home. Our mortgage payment was half of what we had been paying for rent so it was an easy transition for us. Plus, we didn't have any credit card debt!

Living in our first home taught me the most about frugal living. We no longer had a second income to fall back on for car repairs, doctor bills, or any other unexpected expenses. We were also adding to our bills by buying a second vehicle and knowing that we were going to want to upgrade our home in some way as the single wide was literally falling apart around us. We were putting hundreds into it each month just to keep it livable.

We lived in that single wide for 4 years until we came across a deal we couldn't pass up on a double wide. Was a double wide our first option? No, not at all. We would have much rather had a home that was built in the same spot we lived at but it was a way to more than double our living space at a fraction of the cost. At a time when no one was getting a loan, or at least not getting one without a very large down payment, we walked in and were approved that day. That feeling was worth everything we had been through to get there and all of the frugal lessons we needed to learn the hard way.

That double wide was actually an excellent decision. Three years after we bought it, we sold our property with a $16,000 profit. We used this money to pay off one of our vehicles, leaving us with only a truck payment that is due to be paid off in December unless we pay it off earlier. We were able to purchase a larger three bedroom, two bath home on six acres in the location we most desired and at a payment we are comfortable with. Our credit score is now a 742 from a 535. It is possible to climb out of the hole but it takes time and dedication.

This book is a compilation of the real world education my husband and I received so that you can learn from our mistakes. The Frugal Home is split into chapters for many different areas of your life. Instead of trying to fit the entire book to your life, choose a chapter or two and work on adding frugality to that area before moving on to other chapters. Saving money and using resources wisely in one area is going to give you more incentive to extend it to all areas.

The frugal road isn't easy. Many of us will get on it and then get back off several times. My husband and I have gotten on and off the path many times, we learned many lessons during those periods. Take those lessons and get back on the road. Even millionaires can use a few frugal lessons!

Table of Contents

Chapter 1

Beauty and Bath Products

Who doesn't want to look attractive? Most of us want to feel good about ourselves and the way we look. Some people spend hundreds, if not thousands, of dollars a year to make themselves look beautiful. Many do this with no idea that they were actually more beautiful before they began spreading potions and lotions and makeup all over their faces than after, or that they can get the same effect for much less.

Less is Often More When It Comes to Beauty and Bath Products

I was 12 years old when I first realized that I did not need all of these so-called beauty products. Middle school is where all the makeup started and all of the girls began to apply thick blue eye shadow (why do we all always start with blue?) and even thicker foundation. Due to the pimples popping up I also began using any and all acne cleaners that I could. My acne continued to get worse. Since I was already quite nerdy with glasses this just added to my pre-teen embarrassment! The summer before 8th grade I quit using any products on my face and, 'lo and behold, my acne cleared up. To this day, I will occasionally pick up some kind of facial moisturizer and will break out the day after using it. Our skin doesn't need all of these products. If we are healthy, don't smoke, are drinking enough water and using minimal makeup we shouldn't need many, if any, products. If you find you still do, use the minimum amount of product to get the results you want. You may even want to consider a dermatologist to find out what is best for your skin so that you do not have to spend money through trial and error.

Keep Yourself Healthy

Keeping yourself healthy is going to keep you looking good without having to spend a bunch of money to make you look that way. Cutting out sugary drinks and drinking water is not only healthy, but it is going to keep your skin looking its best as well. The better your skin looks, the less you have to spend on expensive lotions for your face.

Take a multi-vitamin to ensure your body is getting the nutrients it needs. This is especially important if you go through a period of time where eating rice and beans is your only option due to a substantial decrease in finances. The multi-vitamin may be the only thing between you and an expensive medical bill.

Eat as healthy as you can. Not only is it more expensive, and it truly is, to eat chips and cookies and processed foods, but it will also cause you more in health insurance and medical bills if you are overweight, if not now then most definitely down the road.

Drink Water

I can't say it enough. Drink more water. You can't get any more frugal, or healthy, than drinking water. Keep a container of water cool in the fridge and carry a BPA-free water bottle around with you to fill up wherever you go. Water keeps you hydrated which will keep both your insides, and your outsides, looking good.

Exercise

When we look good, we feel good, so get out and keep active. Many say that they cannot exercise as it costs too much money but it doesn't have to cost anything at all. It is free to go for a walk or a run and, if you already have the supplies, there are often many areas in town where you can go play a game of basketball or tennis with friends.

FRUGAL TIP
Look for free or cheap ways to get your exercise. Walk or run around your neighborhood or park, jump rope, yoga, do sit-ups or push-ups, play with the kids or dogs, run in place, borrow work-out videos from friends or the library, rent fitness videos from Netflix, do jumping-jacks, yard work, or clean the house.

If you have the money for something more then you may want to look at the cost and usability of a gym membership against at-home gym equipment. Gym memberships can be very expensive so it is best to shop around. You may find a small local gym that costs a fraction of what the larger gyms cost. It is also helpful to find a gym that lets you cancel at anytime, they aren't common but they are out there.

Think about which you will use more. I went to the gym more than I got on my treadmill at home. The treadmill was always there and I always had a chance to get on it, which meant I rarely did. I went with a friend to the gym. I didn't want to let her down so I showed up and I enjoyed taking the classes offered. I had to be there at a certain time and couldn't put it off until that later that never comes. The gym was a more frugal option for me because I used it. If I had used the treadmill more then that would have been the better option. Frugality is never just about what is cheapest but also about what is the best use of your funds. You don't want to spend your resources; both time and money, on a gym membership or a treadmill just because it is the cheaper option, only to never use it.

Chapter 2

The B-Word

No, not that B-word! For many the word budget is as bad as the word diet. As with a diet you don't want to confine yourself within constraints that are too difficult to follow then find yourself quitting and pledging to "start again next Monday".

While there are times when you have no choice but to follow a budget or lose your home or vehicle, if possible it is best to slowly work your way into it. Begin to make small changes that will build to big changes.

Living without a Budget

My husband and I have been together for sixteen years and I took over the finances about six months after we met. It was clear that any money he had in his pocket didn't stay very long, not that I was much better at the time, but I was able to keep my paycheck for a day or two while his was gone within hours. We didn't budget. Our budget consisted of getting a shut-off notice and scrambling to get the money to pay it. We lived in constant fear of debt collectors and that we were going to get kicked out by our landlord or have our electric or water turned off.

Our money went almost completely to entertainment, eating out and going to bars and clubs with friends, or throwing huge barbecues at our home and inviting everyone we knew. It took several years but we eventually stopped the excessiveness. We threw a party one night and people we didn't even know were there eating all of the food and drink we had bought and not one person offered to chip in. We decided then that we were done. Well, almost done.

While we stopped throwing the barbecues, and naturally cut back on the bars and clubs as we got older, we didn't stop the eating out nor did we stop just spending without thought. When we determined we wanted to own a home and made the decision to pay off our credit card debt we knew that creating a budget would get us where we needed to go. It wasn't easy, and we didn't always stick to it, but we got better at it as time went on. We are now so organized that I can tell you what is due on any given week, how much we have for groceries, and we have savings for things such as gifts, tires, clothes, holidays, and new prescription glasses.

How to Create a Budget

Creating a budget can be an overwhelming and emotional experience as you have to get real about the way you have set up your financial life. A budget will not work if you, and everyone who spends money from the family account, are not honest.

Gather together all of your bills and all of your debt. If you owe your mother $20, add it to the pile. A budget is not about only dealing with the bills we want to pay, and ignoring the troublesome ones, but dealing with all of your financial responsibilities from the smallest to the largest.

List every monthly bill such as rent or mortgage, car payments, loan payments, health insurance, school, or utilities.

List the minimum monthly payment for all of your other debt. If your mom says to pay her back when you can then create a monthly payment plan to pay her back.

List how much you spend on food, including eating out and your morning coffee and donut run.

List your yearly payments such as property taxes or car insurance. Then divide it out into how much you need to save monthly to pay those bills when they come due.

List any extras such as entertainment, gifts, clothes, car expenses, etc.

Add all of these numbers together to see how much you have going out each month.

FRUGAL TIP
Breathe deep. Those numbers may be much higher

---

than you expected but facing them is the first step to financial freedom. You may want to breathe deep a couple more times throughout the budgeting process.

Take the amount you have going out each month and subtract this number from the amount of money you bring in each month. Make sure to include all of your income including anything you make off of eBay or child support payments. If you make more than you spend then good for you! If not, then you will have to make some, sometimes serious, adjustments.

Here is a simple breakdown of the numbers needed to make a budget. You may have bills or debt not listed that would need to be added:

Monthly Bills (Home, Car, School, Utilities)
Minimum Debt Payments
Taxes (If yearly, divide out into 12 payments)
Food and Beverages (Don't forget those lattes!)
+ Extras (Entertainment, Gifts, Vacations, Car Repairs etc.)
Total Money Spent a Month
- All Income (Paycheck, Social Security, Ebay, etc.)
Amount left over (if any)

Decide how you are going to pay your bills, whether you will pay them as they come in, weekly, bi-weekly, or monthly. Pay them as you decide. Paying them is the most important part of having a budget! Don't decide to put the electric bill off for a week so that you can go to a concert and then wonder where you will get the money when you get the shut-off notice. That is what you did in your non-frugal life, not what you do now. The new you would already have an entertainment fund set up for just such occasions.

We pay our bills weekly, the day my husband's check is deposited into our primary checking account. I transfer the money needed for bills into another account, savings into our savings account, and what is left stays in the primary account we use for groceries, entertainment, or gifts for the week. Once that runs out we have nothing to spend until the next paycheck.

How to Stick to a Budget

Creating a budget means nothing if you don't stick to a budget so make sure that your budget is realistic. As with a diet you do not want to restrict yourself too much or you will find that you do not follow through. Make small changes and as you feel comfortable add more changes until you are on the financial path you wish to be on.

Instead of going from eating out every day to eating tuna out of a can, you should start small and work your way into something that is comfortable and appropriate for you and your family. Begin by taking your lunch twice a week. Once that becomes easy, add more days until you are taking your lunch as many days as needed to save the amount that will allow you to stick to your budgeting goals. Just make sure that the money you are saving by taking your lunch isn't getting wasted in another area.

Frugal Tip
Saving is an important part of budgeting. Start small if you have to. If you only have $5 a month to save, then start there. Even $5 will eventually add up and, if

you follow a budget and reduce your debt, you will
eventually have more to put back.

There are many methods to help you stick to your
budget but the envelope method and the multiple
bank account method are two that are easy to use by
anyone.

The envelope method entails taking your cash for the
week and separating it out into envelopes marked for
certain areas. You may have an envelope for
entertainment with $30 in it and when you use that
$30 then you are done until the next week. This
allows many to keep track of their money easier,
instead of mindlessly using their debit or credit cards;
they can see in front of them exactly how much money
they have.

While this method works for many it wasn't a method
that worked for us. It was much too easy to take
money out of one envelope and place it into another.
Let's just say that we were not at a point, at that time,
to be honest with even ourselves. Instead of
envelopes, I set up two bank accounts. One was our
general account and the other was used for major bills
only.

My husband's check was direct deposited into the
general account and then we had an automatic
withdrawal to the bill account. This bill account
covered things like our house payment and car
payments. As we do not have debit card access, nor do
we have ATM access to this account, we don't have to
worry about there not being money in there to pay our
most important bills. Once the money in our general
account was gone we were done spending for the

week. This system worked for us for several years and even grew to two other accounts, another checking for other bills, one for business expenses, and a savings account.

Don't be afraid to try several different things, what works for you may not work for me or the neighbor down the street. Whether you use envelopes, bank accounts, or whoopee cushions, what it all comes down to is using what works best for you, your family, and your situation. It doesn't matter how you budget, or what tricks you have to use, as long as you do.

What to Do if You Spend More Than You Make

First things first. Just stop. Stop spending. I know this isn't as easy as it sounds, especially when you are used to going and doing and buying on a whim. My husband and I actually lost friends when we began to quit spending, several friends quit calling once they realized we could only do things like grilling at home and not go out for dinner, drinks, and a club or two. Others were grateful that they then had an excuse to quit spending so much as well.

Once you quit spending begin to cut out items from your budget that you do not need. This is where you have to be honest about wants and needs. Some items are obvious, you know you don't need to eat out every day as you can bring your lunch, and you know that if you bought new jeans last weekend that you don't need new jeans this weekend (unless those were your only pair of jeans!).

Housing is a need; renting a 5 bedroom house when there are only three of you is not. Television is not a need but depending on your job, internet service may or may not be. Soda or beer may seem like needs but water is all you need to live. Honesty at this stage can be very difficult as you may find that talking yourself into spending money is very easy. You may be surprised at how many excuses you can come up with for why you "need" to buy a new car when you could get an older one or continue using the one you have.

If you have cut back all that you can and still find that you have more money going out than coming in you will have to take even more drastic measures. You may have to look at getting a second job or selling items to get your debt down. You may even have to look at your needs and see where you can cut back on them. Perhaps it may be time to look at selling your home for a smaller one with a more comfortable payment, or perhaps you need to sell one of the two cars your family owns in order to get rid of a car payment and insurance payment. Keep reminding yourself, and your family, that sacrifices now will put you in a better financial position in the long run.

Chapter 3

Cleaning With Little Cost

Cleaning is like shelter and food, you really can't do without it and you can only cut back so much before not having it will affect your well-being. At least, I hope this is the case with all of you!

I'm Sensitive to A Lot of Stuff

For us, we didn't just begin to use more frugal cleaning products because we were looking at cheaper options but because I needed to find products that wouldn't cause me to break out in a rash. I began researching more natural cleaning products and was very pleased to find many products that were not only healthier for me and my family, but much cheaper than the products I was using. Many of these products even did a better job than their bleach infused counterparts.

Natural Cleaning

Bleach and ammonia are not your best friends. I have known people who use them on almost every surface of their home. Walking into their house would make you feel like you were swimming in fumes. While each can be a big help when cleaning certain things, after all nothing gets whites whiter, there are many other products that do just as good a job with a great deal less fumes and danger.

Vinegar, baking soda, and Dawn dish soap (the blue one, I don't know why!), are the three main products I keep on hand for cleaning. Vinegar kills bacteria and mold just like those harsh products you are spending a great deal of money on. Baking soda and Dawn dish soap are also great products. A mixture of baking soda and Dawn took all of the soap scum off of a shower that I had spent a lot of time and money trying to clean. I haven't looked back since!

Here is a list of what I use vinegar for:

- Cleaning the toilet
- Spoonful of Apple Cider Vinegar for heartburn
- Clean washing machine
- Unclog a drain by pouring baking soda down the drain and following with vinegar
- Deodorize trash can
- Clean bathroom countertops
- Clean kitchen countertops
- Clean windows

Look online for recipes for natural cleaning products; you probably have most of the ingredients already on hand.

It's Not Just About the Cleaner

I try to buy as few paper towels as I can. Not only are these very expensive, but I also feel a great deal of environmental guilt each time I throw one away. I generally go through about two packages of 8 a year, or a little over one a month. Instead, I bought two packets of cheap dish cloths and I use these as my paper towels. I bought so many so that I can use them like I would use paper towels.

The dish cloths are kept in a basket on my kitchen counter where I can easily grab them for spills or dishes. I then just throw them in the washer. I also use old bath wash cloths for dusting and bathroom cleaning.

FRUGAL TIP
Several years ago I used the fancy mops that took expensive refills but I quit that pretty quick when I realized how much it was costing me to just mop my floor. Now, I just use old wash cloths to mop the floor. They do the job and they're free.

Chapter 4

Digging Out of Debt

Most people find that debt is the main reason they are having trouble making it financially. If they hadn't maxed out their credit cards, and purchased homes and vehicles outside of what they could comfortably afford, then they often wouldn't be in the situation they find themselves in. I know because my husband and I have been there. Don't ever feel judged or ashamed as many have found themselves in the same position as you have. Putting together a plan to get out of debt is the first step to frugal living, building a budget, and becoming more financially responsible.

It's Not Just About Credit Card Debt for Us

I already explained how credit card debt got us into frugal living so I won't bore you by repeating it but I thought I should explain that getting out of debt for us doesn't stop at our credit card debt. We want to get to a point where there is no one that we owe money to. No credit card debt, no car payment, no house payment. This isn't a goal for everyone. Many will be perfectly happy making a car payment and a mortgage payment once they have paid off everything else. There is nothing wrong with this and financial advisors will tell you this isn't necessarily a bad thing either. Our first focus will be to shore up our retirement accounts and once we are comfortable with the amount we are sending to them, we will then begin to pay down the home mortgage. Because of the profit we made on our last house we have paid off our most expensive vehicle and our second will be paid off in less than six months. I have already begun putting money back for when the time comes that we wish to trade in one of our vehicles (this is in addition to saving for any repairs our current vehicles may need). We never want to have a car payment again.

Controlling Debt

If you have debt then you should be controlling it, it should not be controlling you. I know how debt can take over your life. It can take up your every waking thought and stress out you and your family. Taking control of it will help ease the burden.

Controlling your debt means admitting to all of it, down to the five bucks you owe a friend and the store credit card you hide from your spouse. Gather all of your debt, and discuss it with your family if necessary, but also discuss how you plan on fixing it and that while times may be rough for awhile that what you are doing will make your lives financially better off in the long run.

Reduce Your Debt

Controlling your debt will, of course, lead to you reducing it. The road to debt reduction, or getting rid of it all together, has many paths leading to it and many are valid and will get you to the same spot. Here are a few options that I think will work well for people trying to reduce their debt.

Option 1

Make minimum payments but take anything extra (even if it's only $5!) and put it towards one specific debt. This may be your card with the highest interest first or it may be the card with the lowest balance first.

While paying off the card with the highest interest rate first will save you money in the long term, it doesn't always have quite the psychological kick as paying off several debts in a short amount of time. This is what my husband and I did, we felt so great after paying off several debts less than a few hundred dollars that it gave us the boost we needed to go after the bigger debts.

Once you pay off that debt then take its minimum payment and any extra money, and apply it to the next debt. You will find that you quickly begin to pay off your debt without much effort at all. You are creating a debt snowball, essentially, following the Dave Ramsey plan. The amount you are sending to each credit card will get larger and larger.

Option 2

Living on less can be difficult if you are in dire financial straits but if you can, try to save 10% of your income. Use this to build your emergency fund and pay down debt while still making minimum payments. Say you make $500 a week. If you save 10% then you will have an extra $200 a month to go towards building your financial future!

Option 3

You may be looking through your bills and saying that there is no extra money. You can't send extra to any card because you are barely, or not, making payments as it is. You can't live on less because there is no less to live on. Then you may need to think about getting an extra job. Look for something in the evening if your spouse works during the day so someone is home with the children or look for something online so you can stay home. You do not want to create a situation where child care is eating away at your extra income. Remind yourself that you are only doing this to pay off debt and build an emergency fund. Do not begin relying on this extra money as a way to add more debt to your family. Once you have paid off your debt you can quit if you need to or use the money to go on vacations or build your retirement.

Chapter 5

Frugal Decorating

Most of us want to be proud of the homes we live in. However, having a fancy house while racking up the debt, doesn't feel anywhere near as good as a beautiful house and no debt. It is completely possible to live debt free and have a showcase home if you put a little thought into your decorating.

I Love Beautiful Things

I love to have a nice home. I like nice furniture and nice things. I want people to walk in my home and exclaim over an item that they love, whether it's the entire kitchen or a trunk in the bedroom. I have learned over the years that it is very easy to have a beautiful home without spending a great deal of money.

Our home has been decorated with items we have purchased, whether at a retail store or a flea market or a classified ad, items we have made ourselves, items given to us as gifts, and items handed down from family and friends. We love our home and the items in it and we haven't spent a great deal to have it.

Garage Sales, Flea Markets, and Classified Ads

Don't underestimate garage sales and flea markets! You may be surprised at the quality of items you can get if you just put in some time and effort. My husband and I wanted a new entertainment center and we wanted something nice. We shopped flea markets and online classifieds for two months until we found a beautiful three piece set that was being sold for very little as the man selling it needed it gone quickly. This piece would have cost us thousands new and was less than a year old. We used it as an entertainment center for years until we got a flat screen that needed a different setup. Instead of selling the unit we reused it! We put the library ends together in one area and turned the center armoire into a coat and shoe closet for next to our front door.

As we move into our new home we will reuse these pieces again. Since we have a smaller master bathroom than our last house, I will use the bookshelves to hold my jewelry and such while the armoire will house my clothing as the closet is smaller as well. For only $200 we have gotten a great deal of use out of these three pieces and we still have people exclaim over how beautiful they are!

Reuse Your Own Stuff or Others

There are always people who are buying new stuff and getting rid of their old stuff, you may even be one of those people. Reuse what people are getting rid of to decorate your home. Ask friends and family if they are downsizing their furniture. We have gotten some very nice pieces from our parents or friends who were getting new items or had run out of space for other items.

Reuse what you already have as well. While you may be sick of looking at the artwork in your living room that doesn't mean it won't take on new life in another area of your house. I have often taken the décor in my living room and made it the décor in my bedroom or vice versa. Using the art, décor and curtains from one space makes them look completely different in another room.

Frugal Tip
Make your own décor. Much of the artwork in our home was painted by me or my husband. I have also made many of the decorative pillows around the house. If you have ever bought art or throw pillows you know how expensive they can be! Making them at home saves you money and adds an even more personal touch to your surroundings.

Paint

Paint is the frugal decorator's best friend. Paint can change the entire look of a room for very little cost or it can turn dingy old flea market finds into works of art.

I have painted every wall of our home but I have also used paint, and wood stain, to change the look of other aspects of our home. Our kitchen cabinets were a wonderful gold blonde color. And by wonderful I mean horrible. There was no way we could replace the cabinets as we didn't have the funds but we could afford a can of dark stain and some new silver handles. We have gotten many compliments on how modern our kitchen cabinets are while we just smile as we know they were made in the eighties!

Painting furniture, picture frames, and other home décor can take a piece from looking as if it needs to head to the landfill to one that your friends will love. Think about how adding paint or new hardware to an item can help freshen it up when you are shopping at flea markets and garage sales.

I have painted our bedside tables to freshen them up, an old chair, and rod-iron candle holders from my husband's grandmother that we're looking very outdated but by painting them fun colors they took on new life.

Our new home will be a whole new source of frugal decorating. Plans are already being made to strip wallpaper, paint walls and lighting fixtures, and create headboards out of wall coat racks. We will also take our time to find the exact vintage pieces we are wanting as well. Patience is a frugal decorator's best friend. Going out and purchasing all new décor and a living room set at once will cost you much more than taking the time to find less expensive options.

Chapter 6

Entertainment on a Budget

When people begin to look at where their money goes, often they will find that entertaining eats up a great deal of their expenses. Entertainment can be done on a budget, even on a budget where it looks as if you have no money left over for fun.

We Are Entertainment

For us, entertainment on a budget is pretty easy as we enjoy spending time with each other at home. A movie from Netflix and some popcorn almost always sounds appealing to us. We enjoy working outside in the front yard and grilling on the back porch while we watch the dogs play. We do, on occasion, want to get out and do something or spend an evening with friends. We haven't found it difficult to find something cheap, or even free, to do.

Free Entertainment

There is probably a great deal more free entertainment available in your town than you even realize. Many towns have websites with Calendars of Events that let you know when free events are taking place in your town. Look for festivals, concerts, and other events that are completely free to attend. Take our own food and drink in a cooler in the car if you feel you will be there for a long time, or eat before you go so that you do not overspend on food.

Our town has several art festivals for local artists and, not only are they free to attend, but it is much like going to an art museum but with a festival feel! We also have free music concerts and plays throughout the year.

If you don't even have the gas to go out then have fun at home! Have a movie night at home or have the whole family make individual pizzas. Board games may not be as popular as they once were but they are just as fun now as they were then or keep game night current and play more interactive video games such as the Wii. Borrow games from friends or look for them at garage sales to get new games. You can't get much cheaper than a deck of cards and there are more games available than you could ever play.

Call your friends for free entertainment. Perhaps you can have a potluck at each other's houses for some free fun and conversation, or you can meet at a park for a walk or a competitive game of basketball. Our experience has been that the more creative we get with free entertainment the more fun we have.

Cheap Entertainment

Entertainment, even if not free, can be cheaper than you think. Research events in your town and you may be surprised to find that there are many things to do for very little money. We have festivals, discounted movies, or businesses that offer discounted rates on their services during certain times. Our town has a pottery business that lets you create your own pottery for half price on Tuesday afternoons and a movie theater that shows independent films for much less than what is playing at the big movie theaters.

Look for sporting events at your local schools or check out the Minor Leagues in your area. Often they will be much cheaper than the Major Leagues but just as fun.

Often free or at reduced prices during specific times of the week or month, museums are another form of cheap entertainment. This is a great way to get some culture and have an educational activity to do with your loved ones. Many museums will even have areas just for little kids or the entire museum may be geared toward small ones.

Coupons are not just for grocery shopping! Use coupons for your favorite restaurant or entertainment outlet. Taking the time to sign up for a company's newsletter or "club" will often allow you to be sent a great deal of coupons throughout the year that you can use to entertain your family for less.

Frugal Vacations

Vacations don't have to be lavish events that break the bank. Vacations are about getting away from the daily grind and spending time with loved ones. They aren't about not being able to pay the electric bill when you get back.

We have taken several vacations in the 15 years that we have been together. We don't do something big every year but we do try to take time away from work and just have fun together. We have used each of our parents' timeshares to go to Acapulco and Colorado as well as many trips to a resort here in our state. We have also gone on several camping and float trips and created some staycations in which we had a great time just being at home and doing things in our own town.

Staycations have become very popular and don't have to be about just sitting around your house. Camp out in the backyard or buy a small inflatable pool to enjoy for the week. Plan games and get outside with your family. You could even plan a few nights of eating out since you are saving so much by staying home.

FRUGAL TIP
You don't have to go far to have a great vacation. Explore your own state whether it is a short weekend getaway or a full week of vacation. We have found caves, camping, museums, theaters, zoos, botanical gardens, shopping, sports, and many tourist attractions all within our state. We could go on vacation every year for the rest of our lives and still not see it all!

Camping is one of the most frugal vacations you can take. Choose a campground with a lot of entertainment options. Many will have swimming pools, canoeing or kayaking, fishing, and hiking. There are enough activities to keep an entire family busy for a week.

Swap houses with friends or family around the country. They can enjoy all that your town has to offer while you get to see somewhere new. This is especially great if you know someone who lives at the beach and you live in the mountains, or you live in a big city and they live in the country.

Chapter 7

Frugal Food

Of all the areas we can cut out of our budget, food isn't one of them. We may have to eat but we don't have to spend vast amounts of money to do it.

We Gotta Eat

Before my husband and I began to think about our finances differently, it wasn't uncommon for us to spend $100 on a meal and drinks out with friends. We would also purchase groceries and then eat out all week and let all the food in our fridge spoil. I can't tell you how many times I threw out a drawer full of vegetables that had not been looked at once since I put them in there.

Food has been an area that took us some time to learn how best to be frugal in. Even once we had drastically cut back on eating out, we soon found that we were still spending a great deal at the grocery store. It took a few years, and a great deal of trial and error, to figure out how food worked best for us.

Meal Planning and OAMC

After a lot of real world experience, we realized what a significant impact meal planning has had on our food budget. Before I began meal planning, I would just create meals based on whatever sounded good at the moment. We would often not have all of the ingredients for a specific meal, which would mean a side trip to the grocery store, or we would reach the end of the week with nothing more than some limp lettuce and a can of beans.

Once a Month Cooking, or OAMC, is what actually made me appreciate how important meal planning is. I had been reading about OAMC and the idea fascinated me. Cook for a day and eat for a month! How exciting! How brilliant!

How . . . frozen.

As with a lot of ideas I come across on the internet this idea had some aspects that I loved and continue to use, and some that were not suitable for me and my family. I planned out a month of meals that various sites on the internet had assured me would be tasty and just like I had made them fresh that day. It took me an entire day to do the grocery shopping, another day to cook all the food, and another day entirely to clean the kitchen. I was exhausted and by that point had no desire to eat any of the food that I had cooked.

Throughout the month it also became evident that not all OAMC recipes are created equal. Some are awesome; while others, say almost every casserole I have ever tried to make in the last 16 years, are just not something my family will eat. I did learn a great deal in that month though. I learned what freezes well and what doesn't, that a month of freezing is just too much but that several meals or parts of meals are great to freeze, and that planning it out and shopping once or twice a month made a huge impact on our food budget.

I admit I have fallen a bit on the extreme side of meal planning. I have a meal plan set up for two full months of dinners. I do like to eat and two months worth of meals gives me the chance to eat a lot of my favorite meals. I even have a meal plan for the lunches my husband takes to work that I rotate.

It is important to be flexible. If we don't get to a meal, perhaps because we unexpectedly get asked out to dinner, then we just skip it and have it the next round. Meals change as well. Depending on what is in season we may add in different vegetables and fruits. We have even taken meals off and replaced them entirely when we found that we didn't care for them any longer or added options for some meals (for instance, when we are eating a lot of salads for lunch that week and I don't want to have one at dinner as well).

People plan meals in many different ways. Some plan for the week by checking the sales that are currently going on in their area, others rotate two or three weeks of meals in and out, while others, like my family, go for bigger meal plans of a month or more.

However you decide to do it, make a list of your family's favorite meals. I like to leave at least one day in my meal plan that allows for trying something new. Use the plan you create to do your shopping for the week or month.

Make sure that you plan your meals to get the best use of the foods you buy. For instance, we always have leftover roast, and because of this, the day after we always have vegetable beef soup.

You can use your meal plan to create freezer meals but it is important to realize, as I didn't at first, that you don't have to cook an entire month of meals. Freeze just a few meals for busy nights, freeze parts of meals, or make a double batch of your favorite dishes and freeze half for another day. Keeping things in individual sizes (I use my muffin tins for much more than muffins!) will make it easy to grab servings for two or six, depending on whose home for dinner that night.

Here are a few of the foods I freeze that I have found work well for my family's tastes:

Taco Meat – Take out enough meat for a month's worth of taco based meals; we use this meat for tacos, tostadas, taco soup, nachos, and for quesadillas for my husband's lunches. I brown enough ground beef for all of these meals, mix in some salsa and freeze in individual meal portions. Make the taco meat however your family eats it best. We have gluten and dairy allergies so salsa works best for us as a taco seasoning.

Meatballs and Meatloaf – Moist meatballs and meatloaf freeze well. If I make some for dinner I will double or triple the recipe and freeze the extra. Not only is this great for the next time we have meatloaf but I also make them in muffin tins. This makes individual meatloaves that can be reheated on days when we need a quick meal.

Muffins and Cakes – Both muffins, cake, and cupcakes freeze very well. I actually think that freezing them makes them even moister. These are also great for breakfast or to add to a lunch as they thaw quickly. I like to thaw them in a Ziplock bag.

Soups – Most soups will freeze well, though you do have to be careful with certain vegetables, like potatoes or zucchini, which become watery after having been frozen. If there is pasta in the soup I also like to freeze it before the pasta is completely done as it keeps it from falling apart or leave the pasta out and add it the next time I thaw the soup.

Beans – Beans in a bag are much cheaper than beans in a can but they are in no way easier to use. To ensure that I am more likely to buy the cheaper beans in a bag and not reach for the can, I make up a large amount of beans and freeze them in portions I will use. I still keep a few cans of beans on hand for when we need to make a quick meal and don't have time, or don't remember, to thaw frozen beans.

Snacks and Fruit – Having children (or husbands!) in the home means you need a lot of snacks that are healthy yet don't cost a great deal. Kids love frozen fruit. A frozen banana on a stick (roll in chocolate, coconut, or nuts to make it even better) is a tasty snack as are frozen strawberry slices or orange pieces. You can also spread yogurt on graham crackers and freeze, toddlers love this! Make your own trail mix for a healthy, and frugal, option, instead of purchasing it pre-made.

You don't have to freeze food to make things ahead of time. I have pre-made a month's worth of afternoon snacks by placing a cookie, dried fruit, and cheerios into bags; you could pre-make a week's worth of snacks with cut up vegetables and some hummus or peanut butter. When a hungry toddler wakes from a nap or a school-age kid gets off the bus you have something easy to grab. I have also frozen bags with a waffle, grapes, and peaches for quick breakfasts.

Buy in Bulk

Buying in bulk can save you money, as long as you are buying items that will get used or eaten before they go bad. It does no good to buy ten pounds of fresh apples if your family will only eat a few and the rest goes to rot.

FRUGAL TIP
If you do end up with a great deal of one item from a neighbor's garden or a great sale at the Farmer's Market then use them up before they go bad by freezing them into meals or snacks. Apples can be made into apple pie filling, apple bread, apple butter, or apple sauce. Zucchini can be made into bread or frozen shredded or cubed to be used in pastas or soups. Only buy in bulk if you can come up with ways of storing the food until you can use it whether that is in your cabinet or frozen.

Buying in bulk works for things like rice, flour, or other staples, unless, of course, you have a large family. You should also have a great deal of storage space available if you are planning to buy in bulk or you will end up with containers of dried beans underneath your bed.

If you are buying in bulk from a warehouse make sure that you are saving enough, and using it enough, to make up for the fact that you have to pay an annual fee to shop at the warehouse store.

Eat What Is In Your House

We all know this isn't as easy as it sounds. How many times have you thrown out old rotten vegetables or found leftovers in the back of the fridge, weeks after you remember cooking it? Rotten food is wasted money.

Making a meal plan will help keep you from wasting food but if you find you have a lot of leftovers that are not being eaten you may want to try freezing them for TV dinner nights or have a leftover night a few times a month to use up what is in your fridge. It also doesn't hurt to rethink how you use items. We have been out of lettuce before but had plenty of cabbage and used it instead for tacos. They still tasted great!

Don't forget soups! If you have vegetables about to go bad cut them up and throw them in a pot for vegetable soup. I will also use them to throw in the pot when I am making chicken or beef broth. Even if you do not eat it that day you can freeze it for lunches or a rushed dinner.

Eat Healthy

Many people think that frugal eating has to mean unhealthy eating and it doesn't. You will often hear how junky, processed food is cheaper but this isn't true. A bag of carrots and a bag of apples do not cost much and will stretch much further than a bag of chips. Dried beans and rice aren't expensive either.

For items that do cost a little more look at ways of obtaining them for less:

Instead of buying your fish at the store, head to your nearest river or lake and catch your own.

Plant a garden. Even a few herbs on your windowsill can save you money.

Visit the Farmer's Market in your town, which also helps the local economy.

Work on a farm. There are community farms that allow you to work for a set amount of hours in exchange for a specified amount of vegetables each week.

Can or freeze fruits and vegetables when they are in season

Eat in season for cheaper fruits and veggies. Don't be afraid to step outside your potatoes and corn box!

Not only can eating healthy be frugal but by eating less you will save money not only on your grocery bill but also in medical bills, and losing weight will cost you less in health insurance.

Choose One Meat for the Week

While this is easy to do for dinner, I actually do this for my husband's lunches. Each week is a different meat and I plan his lunches around that week. You could plan the meals around what is on sale or put the meats on a rotation to ensure variety. For his lunches, I make up all of his lunches for the week on Sunday and place them in plastic storage in the fridge so all I have to do is throw it in his lunch bag the night before. If it is a meal that can be frozen I will freeze several ahead of time for even easier lunch making.

Example Meals with Chicken

> Chicken Quesadillas
> Grilled Chicken on a Salad
> Chicken Salad Sandwich
> Chicken and Rice
> Asian Lettuce Bowls

Example Meals with Ground Beef

> Ground Beef Quesadillas
> Hamburger
> Pasta
> Meatball Sandwich
> Sloppy Joes
> Taco Wrap or Salad

Frugality with Food Allergies

If you or someone you know has food allergies then you understand how expensive those items can be when they are free of your specific allergen.

I am both gluten intolerant and I have a dairy allergy. Many of the products, such as dairy free cheese, or (good!) gluten-free bread are very expensive. After a great deal of trial and error I figured out which products I enjoy the most and I stock up when they are on sale. There are also often coupons available if you contact the company.

Some items I just do without more often than not. When I was first diagnosed with a dairy allergy there were almost no great tasting milk alternatives so I got used to living without. Even though there are now decent dairy free cheeses available, I still eat my pizza without cheese and when I became gluten intolerant I began eating my hamburgers without a bun. These changes meant that I could use the expensive products for areas in which they were more important, such as dairy free sour cream for my tacos or gluten free brownies. You may have to make some sacrifices to have the allergy free products you enjoy most.

Frugal Meal Ideas

Here are a few of the frugal meals my family enjoys:

Breakfast
Oatmeal topped with berries or cinnamon
Sausage patties on a toasted English muffin
(cheaper than fast food and better tasting! You can even freeze them!)

Lunch
Wraps and quesadillas of all kinds

Peanut butter and jelly (can't beat an old standby!)

Leftovers from the night before

Soups

Salads

Dinner

Cottage Pie with Colcannon Topping – This is comfort food at its finest! I like to mix finely diced carrots, celery and onion in with the browned ground beef (you can also do ground turkey). Pour a can of creamed corn over the ground beef mixture then top it with Colcannon, an Irish dish consisting of mashed potatoes mixed with cabbage or kale. While the cabbage is good the kale just can't be beat! Top with butter and bake.

Spaghetti – Make a double batch and freeze half of it to use for baked spaghetti another day. Add shredded zucchini and carrots to the spaghetti or any pasta with red sauce to up the health content.

Slow Cooker Chicken Parts – Chicken parts are very cheap and are a great way to make an easy dinner. Throw them in a slow cooker with your favorite herbs and spices or a bottle of salsa for an easy dinner. Throw over rice or serve with a salad or make into tacos, pastas, or casseroles.

Tuna and Chickpea Salad – Throw together a can of tuna, two cups chickpeas (garbanzo beans), half a green pepper and half an onion chopped up. Mix olive oil, Italian seasoning, and lemon juice to taste and throw everything together with romaine (or any kind) of lettuce. This is a great cheap and healthy meal!

Chapter 8

Grocery Shopping

Grocery shopping is another one of those things that we just can't do without, unless of course you grow your own food, but that just isn't the case for the overwhelming majority of us. Even those with large gardens will often still spend a great deal at the grocery store each year.

I Love Grocery Shopping

I really do love grocery shopping. Since I work from home it is sometimes the only time I get out into town and into clothes other than shorts or sweats and a t-shirt. I also enjoy the thrill of checking things off my list and finding an extra good deal. I love coming home, unloading and putting everything away. Even though I'm usually exhausted after a trip, as it isn't uncommon for me to visit three or four stores in one day, I love the feeling that our fridge, freezers, and pantries are full and that we could easily eat for at least a month, probably two or three.

Coupons

Coupons are a great way to save money for a lot of people. There are numerous websites available that will teach you how to use coupons to save the most money. Personally, I do not use them very often. Due to the food allergies in our home and that we try to eat healthy and have a minimum of processed foods, many of the coupons are not useful for us. For things like toiletries I have not found that I saved enough to cover the cost of buying ink for my printer or purchasing newspapers. If I come across a coupon that doesn't cost me anything to use then I will gladly use it, otherwise I shop sales and discount grocers such as Aldi. For many families though, couponing saves them thousands of dollars a year. Coupons can also be loaded to a lot of store cards now so you don't have to print them or buy a newspaper.

Sales and Circulars

Grocery stores put out weekly circulars advertising the items they have on sale for that week. The day those circulars come out, I check them online and use them to make my weekly grocery list.

Many people keep a price list either in their head or on paper. I have an app on my phone that allows me to keep track of prices. This allows me to figure out what the best deals are in the circulars and purchase accordingly. For instance, we can only eat a few brands of margarine as they have to be both gluten and dairy free. When I see it go on sale, which isn't often, I know to buy ten or twelve containers and freeze them so that we have enough to last us until the next sale. Buying like this is why you need extra storage, both in the pantry and in the freezer.

Pantry Shopping

This can be taken two ways. Pantry shopping can mean creating meals out of what is already in your pantry. This is a great option if you are not able to make it to the grocery store this week or to make sure that you are using the food you bought in bulk. Instead of heading to the grocery store, make up something out of what you already have on hand.

I also look at pantry shopping another way. I don't grocery shop specifically for the next week's meals. Instead, I buy the foods that we use regularly as they come on sale, hence, shopping for my pantry. Since we aren't starting from scratch this works well for us.

One week I may purchase sale items like chicken breasts, green beans, and gluten free pizza dough or another week may be nothing but canned tomatoes and frozen broccoli. We may not actually eat any of those items for another month. I do this because when their turn does come up in the meal plan I don't have to worry if they are going to be on sale or not. This, of course, excludes items that spoil and need to be bought as needed such as fresh fruits and vegetables.

Pantry shopping in this way means that we are almost always buying items that are on sale and rarely paying full price.

Discount Food Chains and Warehouse Stores

We use both but they aren't for everyone. We have an Aldi in our town, which is a great discount food chain if you have one. They keep their prices cheap through their own suppliers, an efficient business product, and fewer options than your normal grocery stores. I buy the bulk of our food at Aldi after quickly realizing years ago that I was saving at least half, if not more, of our grocery budget just by purchasing the same items at Aldi as I would at other stores.

Some people say that they save more by combining sale ads and coupons. For us that just didn't work though I know for many families it can. You have to figure out which method works best to save your family the most money.

Warehouse stores are another area that can save money for some and not so much for others. Large families can benefit at warehouse stores, as well as families that can have storage to stock up on items. The downfall is thinking you are getting a deal. Like I said before, if you buy ten pounds of apples but only eat two or three then you haven't saved money, you have only thrown it away. Also, make sure that the amount you are saving is more than the yearly membership fee.

Meal Planning

Meal planning was also discussed in the Frugal Food chapter but it bears repeating in the Grocery section as well. Meal planning will turn your grocery shopping trips into a breeze. Just look at what is already planned for the week, go through your pantry and fridge to see what you already have on hand, and make a list with what is left, or pantry shop for the items you will need that are on sale.

This takes so much of the stress out of grocery shopping and makes for easy shopping list creation. I use our meal plan to grocery shop up to a month ahead of time. Very little thinking involved, just add to the list what isn't already in the house, it is super easy since I already know exactly what ingredients I will need, even for a meal three weeks from now!

FRUGAL TIP
Shop for loss leaders – items that stores deeply discount to get people in the store and hopefully buy items that are not discounted. Of course, this only works if you don't buy a bunch of other stuff you don't need!

Making a list for your grocery shopping trip will help you save money, *if* you stick to the list. Unless there is a great deal on an item that you use regularly, do not get sucked into the newest product or sales that look like they are great but really aren't. Post a notepad on the fridge, and anytime someone runs of something or notices an item getting low they can add it to the list. By the time the grocery run comes around, you will already have a partial list made.

Chapter 9

Health Care Is Cheaper Than Not Having Health Care

Health care is expensive. It is right up there with your most costly bills but, just like your rent or mortgage, it is more of a necessity than you may think.

I Was Without Insurance for Eight Years

When I quit my job years ago to return to school, I not only lost my income but I also lost my health insurance. The income loss also meant there was no way I could afford to pay for insurance myself. Lucky for me, I was lucky. I was young, generally healthy, and very rarely got sick.

And then I started to get older. I knew I needed some tests done but couldn't afford them and there were a few times when I was so sick that I sent my husband to his doctor with my symptoms so that I could get antibiotics. He has always had insurance through his job and we looked at adding me to his insurance but it would have cost us about four hundred extra dollars a month. That was almost as much as our house and land payment!

I stuck it out for years, hoping nothing serious would go wrong. Then, a few years ago, my husband began to have major back problems. We spent thousands of dollars in one year alone on his medical issues, even with his insurance. I knew then that if something like that happened to me that we could easily be put into thousands of dollars of debt.

I began searching until I found an insurance that would cover my basic needs at a price we could afford. Six months later I had a breast cancer scare and had to have several tests done. At that time I realized how grateful I was to have insurance.

I won't go into the politics of health care; all I do know is that even the most basic of coverage can keep you from paying thousands of dollars in medical bills.

FRUGAL TIP
Quit smoking. You don't have to tell me how hard it is. I did it five years ago and it was one of the hardest things I have ever done but it was also one of the best. Quitting smoking will free up a great deal of your extra cash, it will lower your insurance premiums, your dental bills will go down, and you won't be anywhere near as sick. I used to get bronchitis every year but I haven't had it since the year I quit smoking. If you follow no other advice I give in

---

It is a Must Have

Health insurance is a must have. It isn't like cable that you can do without, or even a car when you can use public transportation or share with your spouse. Not having health insurance can cause you to incur serious debt, perhaps even hundreds of thousands of dollars in debt.

Look for Affordable Health Care

It may sound like an oxymoron but it's true, you can find affordable health care. It may not cover everything you may need but it can keep you from having to file bankruptcy from tens of thousands of dollars in medical bills.

I pay less than $200 a month for health insurance. I no longer have to just suffer through an illness, I can go get antibiotics. When my doctor found the lump in my breast, I didn't even have to worry about how much the tests would cost, nor did I worry when I had to have my thyroid or my cholesterol tested, two tests I probably would not have had done had I not had insurance. My husband no longer has to worry that if something happens to me and I get sick, that we don't have some kind of coverage.

Keep Yourself Healthy

Keeping yourself healthy is the key to keeping your health care costs down. I get charged an extra $30 a month because I was overweight when I signed up. An unhealthy lifestyle will cost you more money, if not now then down the road. If you keep healthy you will have less doctor visits, less illness, less time off of work, and you will keep your premium lower than your overweight peers.

Chapter 10

Have a Frugal Holiday or Event

Nothing is quite a budget buster like a nice holiday or family event. We tend to ignore our overspending when it comes to buying a nice gift for, or having a good time with, our friends and families but it doesn't have to be this way. You can create a holiday or an event for very little money without anyone having to know how much you actually spent!

I Love Holidays, Events Not So Much

I do love the holidays. I enjoy birthdays, Halloween, any holiday that revolves around the barbecue grill, Thanksgiving and Christmas. I love spending time with my family and friends and the general festivity that goes along with it. I'm not big on weddings or showers of any kind or most other events. You will be invited to at least one, if not all, of these at some time in your life so I do have to make the most of it even if the thought of playing games with a baby bottle is not how I want to spend my Saturday afternoon. If you are like me, just remember that there was someone who didn't want to be at your event but came with a smile on their face anyway!

We always seemed to be extra poor right around a holiday or event, or perhaps we were just always broke and there are so many holidays and events, especially as most big yearly bills come around the holidays with such things due as taxes and insurances. Either way, we had to get the most bang for our buck, and we got to be very good at it. It took several years but we learned best how to plan holidays and have the money available to purchase gifts for those we care about.

Gifts

Gifts are often the most expensive area in regards to holidays or special events but they are also the best place to cut back on your holiday budget.

Homemade gifts may seem cheap, or it may seem like others would not like them, but you may be very surprised! We love getting homemade gifts. We have had a great deal of furniture made for us, from a kitchen island made by my husband's parents to an end table made by my sister and brother-in-law refurbished from a table my mom made in high school. We have also been given homemade soup mixes, jars of pickles, quilts, and other great homemade gifts.

You don't have to create it yourself to give a quality, low-price gift. There are a great deal of items you can get for under ten dollars from magazine subscriptions (a gift that keeps on giving), scarves, gift cards (make it 2 $5 cards for more fun), coffee mugs filled with sweets like chocolate dipped pretzels, board games (yes, those old-fashioned games that don't involve batteries or the television!), journals, gloves, a package of light bulbs, holiday décor or ornaments, or fashion jewelry.

Talk to your family and discuss the gift exchanges for the year. Perhaps everyone would like a break from buying for anyone but their own immediate family or perhaps everyone would rather go on a vacation or weekend getaway together as opposed to a bunch of presents.

Saving for the Holidays

Saving for the holidays shouldn't start the same month that the holiday is in. Decide at the beginning of the year what your holiday budget is going to be. Make sure that you think about all of the holidays (you will probably want fireworks on the Fourth of July, a barbecue on Memorial and Labor Day, eggs and new clothes for spring, and costumes and candy for Halloween), events, and birthdays throughout the year. We also like to throw in a little extra in case we get invited to a wedding or housewarming and need to bring a gift; if the amount isn't used then it is just extra for Christmas or New Year's!

Once you have come up with an amount you will need for the entire year, divide it equally among your paychecks or turn it into a "bill" that you pay each month into your savings.

Get the Entire Family Involved

It can be easier if you get your entire family involved with having a less expensive holiday. Explain to your immediate family what you are trying to do and have them offer suggestions or options, such as a larger family gift (like a game console) and one small personal gift or three small gifts. Then speak with your extended family and discuss having a potluck holiday get-together or converse about other ideas on which you can save money during that particular holiday or event.

Buy After the Holiday

It may seem backwards but buying after the holidays can save you a great deal of money!

After December – Stock up on wrapping paper, gift bags, tape, holiday décor, chocolate for Valentine's Day, and ornaments. Purchase solid, non-holiday colored, wrapping paper and gift bags, such as blues or yellows, which can be used throughout the year for birthdays, anniversaries, or other events where you need to bring a gift. I also like to pick up any décor or ornaments after the holidays to use myself the next year or to give as gifts. I have purchased many ornaments and decor for less than a dollar after the holidays and given them as gifts the next year or used them as an extra gift to bulk up a smaller present. I love to purchase a new ornament each year for our family and I am able to get a much nicer ornament after the holidays than before. This is also a great time to purchase the supplies for next year's New Year's Eve party as well.

After Valentine's Day – Chocolate and candy! I will often buy my husband his Valentine's chocolate after the holiday as he gets much nicer chocolate for much less. I will also stock up and parcel out chocolate and candy for weeks after. This is another great time to get red, pink, or white décor for your home or to give as gifts. Candles often go on sale in Valentine's colors and make for a great wedding or housewarming gift!

After Easter – Stock up on ham! Ham will often go on sale both before and after the Easter holiday. Use this time to buy extra and freeze it to use throughout the rest of the year. Also, purchase baskets for use around the house or to use the next year and décor in Easter colors (great for baby showers!).

After Memorial Day/Labor Day – Grab up those red, white and blue linens to be used on the Fourth of July or for any outdoor barbecue.

After the Fourth of July – If you have a safe place to keep them then buying fireworks the day after the Fourth is much cheaper than buying them the day before. We used to buy all of our fireworks the day after and got double what we would get the day before.

After Halloween – Costumes! Halloween costumes will be a fraction of the cost if bought after as opposed to before. Just make sure that you buy something like a witch or a Spiderman costume that will still be popular the next year where something like Dora or Bob the Builder may be old news to your little one. If, as an adult, you know that you will wear the same outfit each year you may want to splurge on a better made costume (such as Renaissance costumes) that you can wear year after year. If you eat a lot of candy then this is the time to stock up. Even if you don't, look at purchasing some and making little gift bags as a gift to anyone who may drop in during the holidays, as a gift at Thanksgiving dinner, or as a host/hostess gift as you visit throughout the holiday season. Just choose candy or chocolate that will last and is not Halloween themed. All of our Halloween décor has been purchased for at least half price after the 31st.

After Thanksgiving – As with all the other holidays, Thanksgiving décor is best purchased after the holiday. I have purchased both Thanksgiving and Halloween décor that is more fall themed than holiday themed and I use it to decorate my home for the entire season. I also like to grab my linens for the next year and any food products that go on sale that we will use around Christmas.

Holiday Entertaining

Entertaining for a holiday or event is often much more expensive than the gifts we purchase. Make it a challenge, plan with your family and friends to have fun without spending a great deal of money.

Have someone in your family dress as Santa Clause. Not only is this fun but you will get those great Santa pictures for much less! This is a costume you would want to purchase after Halloween or Christmas. Get a good one and it will last for years of fun!

Have everyone bring their favorite board game for some family fun that is much better than parking everyone in front of the TV.

Budget how many parties you can attend and buy only one or two outfits (that can be interchanged) to wear to all of them. You may also look at cutting back on the number of parties you attend; you don't have to say yes to them all!

Get your music on the download! There are a lot of free holiday songs and many of them are upbeat and fun.

Christmas

One of the biggest arguments around Christmas revolves around purchasing a real or a fake tree. Personally, I say go for the fake tree unless you have a Christmas tree you can cut down out of your back yard and even then I'd still get a fake one! We have a lot of allergies in our home, and our green thumbs aren't that green, so a fake tree just works better for us. Until recently, our artificial trees came as hand-me-downs from family. We then bought one after Christmas that was larger as our home had gotten larger.

If you do purchase a real tree then try to recycle it afterwards. Many towns will pick them up for mulch. If you need to get rid of an artificial tree, sell it on your town's online classifieds or donate it to someone who wouldn't have a tree otherwise.

Ornaments or holiday décor can make great Christmas gifts, especially for gift exchanges or as a gift for someone who unexpectedly shows up. If you bought them after the holidays the year before it is even better!

Spend time with your family instead of buying each other gifts. Give each other gifts of time, whether it is a gift of spending an afternoon shopping with your mother or the gift of watching your sister's children while she gets some time to herself.

Have an appetizer Christmas dinner and recipe exchange. We have done this in my family and we all loved it. Everyone brings two appetizers. We make them together and have them for Christmas dinner instead of the normal ham or turkey dinner. We loved tasting what each person brought and we still got to spend time together in the kitchen.

We also have a recipe exchange. The girls bring recipes for the girls and the boys bring recipes for the boys. Along with the recipe we attach one ingredient from the recipe. You may have a recipe for cookies and attach them to a bag of chocolate chips or a recipe for egg rolls attached to a bottle of oil. This is a great gift exchange idea for large families!

We used to try to do a bunch of activities when we were all together but soon realized that we just wanted to spend time together. Now we may play some games or watch a movie but mostly we sit around and visit with each other. We have found that this is our favorite way of spending the holidays with our families.

Thanksgiving

Thanksgiving is one of my favorite holidays and I host it every year for our families. My planning for this holiday begins over two months before it rolls around. I plan out the menu in detail with my traditional recipes and I always try to make one new item. We alternate Thanksgiving's with each of our families, one year it is mine and the next it is my husband's. We have discussed having everyone each year but I like having the personal time with each family and I think it would be a bit overwhelming to have both families at once!

Generally our family (whichever side is coming that year) brings the desserts as that isn't my thing. Partly because the food allergies keep me from being able to eat what the others can eat and partly because I would rather have two plates of Thanksgiving dinner than dessert! Give me my turkey and sweet potatoes!

I begin to purchase the non-perishable items for our Thanksgiving dinner in September and buy a little each week so that we do not have to come up with the money for the meal all at once, it ends up being only about ten dollars extra on our grocery bill. If that is even too much on your budget then think about creating a potluck Thanksgiving dinner. Offer to make the turkey and have everyone bring their favorite side. Just make sure you get the menu from everyone before the big day as you don't want three people bringing pumpkin pie and no one bringing rolls or mashed potatoes.

Keep the menu as simple as possible for your Thanksgiving dinner to keep within a budget. Here is a sample frugal Thanksgiving menu:

Turkey or Ham
Mashed Potatoes or Sweet Potato Casserole
Green Bean Casserole or Green Beans
Roasted Vegetables or Salad

Rolls

We like to get a bigger bird than we need for the amount of people we will be serving so that we can send leftovers home (buy some cheap plastic storage containers so that your family and friends can take some home with them) and so that we can use the leftovers to make some great freezer meals like turkey pot pie or turkey vegetable soup.

Potatoes are cheap and are a great way to bulk up your meal. Our potatoes change based on our finances. We have made mashed potatoes with some of the turkey broth and what butter we could scrape out of the container if that was all we had the money for, while other times we have had mashed potatoes with cream cheese and sour cream, topped with green onions and bacon, and baked in the oven with a sweet potato casserole on the side. You do as much or as little as you can, it all tastes good that day whether you have ten dishes or three!

Green bean casserole or green beans can be left out of the menu if needed but they are a great traditional addition if you can afford it. The best is if you have frozen some from your garden that summer as then you wouldn't have to spend any money!

Roasted vegetables or a salad can be inexpensive if you make them with cheaper vegetables. Even just roasting some carrots in balsamic vinegar will make an elegant, and low cost, side dish.

Just about everyone wants some kind of bread at Thanksgiving and making homemade rolls is a great frugal alternative. If you don't have the ingredients then buying a bag of the cheapest sandwich bread would be an option. Throw some butter on the table and watch everyone dig in!

Thanksgiving isn't just about the food for me. I love to set my dining room table and will often have it set up a week beforehand just so that I can look at it. My Thanksgiving dishes have been mostly bought from antique stores and flea markets over the years and a few have been given to me from family. They don't all match but I love each and every dish. I may have spent fifteen dollars on all of it as most of the dishes cost as little as 25 cents each.

Last year I bought a beautiful gold tablecloth on sale after Halloween but I have used a white sheet before that worked out beautifully and no one even noticed! I now have a Thanksgiving centerpiece that I bought on sale after Thanksgiving one year but in previous years we either did without or I created one with a glass bowl and colorful beans with candles stuck down in it or bowls filled with water that I floated flowers in (artificial ones from my craft stockpile).

I like to add place cards as well and I make these with whatever craft supplies I have available or I make something on the computer and just print them out. I like to have favors as well. I have done candy in little boxes that I got on sale for pennies or cupcakes at each person's plate.

Thanksgiving isn't just about the dinner; it is about spending time with your family. Entertainment can be completely free. Take a walk or play football outside after dinner. Play dice or cards. Get out the active game console and have everyone play, even the Grandparents. Watch the football game. Sit around, talk and catch up with everyone. Have fun but don't worry about spending any money!

Chapter 11

Bargain Basement Kids

We are pretty new to the parenting game but we learned quickly that kids are expensive. Very expensive. Finding frugal ways of raising them without them looking and feeling like a bargain basement kid can take some creativity.

Our First Kiddo

We do not currently have children but we did foster a little boy for over half a year that taught us much about frugality and children, not to mention the rest that he taught us!

Clothes and Toys and Such

To be honest, you can find everything you would ever need for a child at garage sales and in the classifieds. There are even websites for parents to swap or sell children's clothes. You can also look on sale racks where you may find entire outfits for just a few dollars. Don't forget to check Goodwill or the Salvation Army for clothing as well. They will often have great stuff; you just may have to dig through it a bit!

Social networking sites are another great resource for parents. Send out a call to your friends for any items you may need. You may just find that other parents are more than willing to part with their items.

Kid Fun

Sometimes it can seem like the only thing that will entertain your child costs a great deal of money, but if you look around your town and home you will probably find plenty to keep them occupied.

At home, small kids love to play with dishes (anyone want to bang on a pot with a wooden spoon?) and older kids love to help you cook. Start a small garden, whether inside or out. Make crafts with whatever is around your house, even a paper towel cardboard roll and some crayons can be used to get the imagination going. I have even taken a box and drawn wheels and windows on it for the little one to use as a race car. Once he was done it went in the recycling, he got to play with something new and clean up was a snap!

FRUGAL TIP
Kids love spending time with their parents more than anything else (even those teenagers who act like they want nothing to do with you!). Have frugal outings with personal time just for you and your child to have a picnic,

---

play a game, or just sit and talk. Put the phone down! They will love that you are just focusing on them and not everything else that is going on in your life.

Check your local city events calendar or local websites for free or cheap fun. Our town has dollar movie days for kids, free splash parks, outdoor concerts, events where kids can see fire trucks and climb on them, and all kinds of fun, and free, things to do for the whole family.

Cheap Snacks

If you are buying packaged snacks, chances are you are spending too much and it isn't very healthy anyway. We have come up with a lot of cheap and healthy snacks for kids.

Freeze fruit. Bananas cut in half and put on a popsicle stick make for a great treat (especially rolled in chocolate or nuts!) as do many other fruits. I freeze strawberry, orange, grape, and peach slices and our little one loves to nibble on them.

I make an afternoon snack bag for after nap or it could be used for after school. It has two small cookies, a handful of cheerios, a few nuts, and a few pieces of dried fruit. I may pay ten bucks for all of it and once separated out it gives me an afternoon snack bag every day for a month.

Wraps are great snacks. Roll up some cream cheese and green pepper slices or chicken and lettuce. You can even change up the old stand-by and put your PB&J on a tortilla instead of on a piece of bread.

Cut up some veggies and serve them with homemade hummus or the dressing of your choice. Our kiddo likes sliced green peppers and broccoli. Try different vegetables until you find what your kid likes the best. Carrots and celery would be some of the cheapest vegetables you could purchase and would make a great snack.

Popcorn is another cheap snack if your youngster is old enough for it. Buy plain popcorn and, instead of drowning it in butter (don't act like you haven't!), sprinkle on your favorite popcorn seasoning recipe.

Chapter 12

Save the Earth on a Budget

Many feel that going green isn't important, costs too much, or just isn't something they have the time for. You can change just a few simple things to make your home more environmentally friendly that will cost you less money overall, will take up little to no space, and are very easy to add into your household routine.

Create a Garden

A garden can be created anywhere, whether you live in a small apartment or a large country home.

Small apartments can grow window or balcony container gardens. Carrots, green onions, spinach, and a wide variety of herbs are all great options for container gardening. These can give you fresh vegetables even if you just set a couple containers behind your kitchen sink. Even though we have a few acres of land, I still grow herbs in my windows so that I have fresh herbs year round and I can grab what I need as I'm cooking.

If you have the room you can put in a large garden and grow enough for fresh fruits and vegetables for your entire family. It may take you a few years to learn what you grow best as well as what your family eats the most of, and what they don't eat much of (though I do love getting the excess when our family members plant too much of something!). Don't forget that you can freeze or can many foods that you cannot eat fresh.

Recycling

Most recycling is easy and free. This makes it one of the best ways you can save the Earth on a budget. Recycle your cans, paper, and plastic, anything that you can recycle in your town. For items that may cost to recycle, look for free recycling days or take the items to places that will take them as donations.

We have extra trash cans set up in our closets just for recycling and to make it easy to separate items out. Our town has drop-off points in several areas where you can leave your recycling, or, if you live in town there is often a recycling day just like there is a trash day and you can set your recycling on the curb for the city to pick up.

Reduce

Another easy ways to save the Earth is to quit spending so much. Cook at home, cook from scratch, and recycle to reduce the amount of trash you send to the landfill. A compost pile will help you reduce the amount of trash you send out as well as giving you great compost for your garden. Composting alone reduced our trash bags by one bag a week.

Look at all of your spending to find ways to reduce. Do you really need another black pair of pants or do you have several pairs at home that would work? You probably don't need a new pair, after all they are black pants; no one is going to notice you wore the same pair last week. Do you throw out rotten vegetables or leftovers at the end of the week? If you aren't going to eat it then buy less or learn to use it up or freeze it before it goes bad.

Reuse

Reuse what you already have. Glass jars can be used instead of plastic containers, old clothes or rags can be made into quilts or cleaning rags, and gift bags can be reused if they aren't beat up in the opening process.

We have reused a great deal of items, including furniture. A bedroom set from my Great-Grandfather has been used by my parents, me, and my sister. Once no one needed the actual set any longer I took the dresser again, painted it black, added new crystal knobs, and turned it into my dining room buffet.

Utilities

Most of us would like to save money on our utilities and in doing so we are automatically being environmentally friendly. Have an energy audit done on your house so that you can see where you may be losing heat through your home. Reduce drafts around windows or doors, even the walls in some houses. I was very surprised to look down just before getting in the shower one day, to find that I could see directly under our house through a small hole in our floor. No telling how much that little hole cost us and probably explained why that room always had such a different temperature from the room next to it!

Put in a programmable thermostat and keep it as warm in the summer or as cool in the winter as you can. Remember, always take clothes off in the summer or put more clothes on in the winter before deciding that it is not cold or warm enough. Make the change gradually. We went from having the cold air set at 70 in the summer and worked our way up to 78. Most days this is perfectly comfortable. We saved about $600 a year just by making these changes.

Search the internet for other ways to save on your utilities such as covering your windows in winter or keeping all the lights off during the day. Call your utility company as well, most offer energy audits for free or very little.

Vehicles

Fuel efficient cars are not only good for the environment but they will also cost you much less in gas. This is especially important as gas will just keep getting more expensive. If possible try to get by with just one vehicle for your family, instead of two or more, or not have a car at all.

I have read several articles about getting rid of your cars and relying only on public transportation. For us, and I would imagine for a great deal of Middle

America and elsewhere, this just isn't possible. We live in the country and there is no public transportation out here. We have gotten by on one car off and on for many years. It isn't always easy but it has been necessary and has helped us get onto a better financial path.

Chapter 13

Taking Care of Your Home and Yard

It can seem overwhelming, and expensive, when we look at all of the things that need to be done around our home and how much it would cost to do it all. This is where living a frugal life can be a huge help!

Creating a Frugal Yard and Home

As I stated previously, our two and a half acres had a single wide placed on it when we first purchased the property. An elderly woman lived in it before we bought it and the front yard was large with some randomly placed bushes and flower groupings while the back was fenced with a dilapidated shed and one lonely Yucca plant placed in the middle. Lucky for us, in some ways, an abundance of water surrounded our property and we never had a lack of bright green grass.

Our property went through many manifestations while we lived there, the least of which was moving from a single wide to a double wide. We, at differing times, had a back deck and a front deck, no decks, decks without rails, a swimming pool with a deck, a garden, a two bay garage, large trees, dead trees, a hill full of flowers, and an old bridge. In its final manifestation before we sold it, this home had three decks off of our double wide, the swimming pool was taken down and turned into a fire pit and patio, the front yard boasted a white picket fence around a playground with a stamped concrete patio and sidewalk lined with hostas, we added a new bridge, and the two bay garage was extended to four. We learned a lot
about creating, and taking care of, a frugal home and yard.

Garden

Gardens can be expensive to start so look to neighbors and friends to help you begin. Borrow a tiller from a neighbor or ask around to see if anyone has any extra fencing or chicken wire that they want hauled off their property to use to enclose your garden and keep animals out.

Check out online websites such as freecycle.org or craigslist.com to see if anyone is giving away anything you could use. Someone may have purchased too many pepper plants or something and just want you to take them away.

Landscaping

If you head to your local garden store you will find
that the price on landscaping can quickly get out of
hand but if you plan correctly you can create a very
frugal landscape.

Again, freecycle.org and craigslist.com, or similar, are
two great websites to search for free or cheap
landscaping supplies. People will often offer large
amounts of dirt or paving stones, or other landscape
supplies, if you just go and pick it up off of their
property. These things are usually heavy so it is
important to have access to a truck and some strong
backs but you could cut your costs to almost nothing
next to the thousands you would spend if purchased
in a store.

Be willing to take time to build your yard and make
adjustments based on what is available as well as what
you are capable of doing yourself. If you can shovel a
truck bed full of dirt then do so but if you can't then
you will have to find someone else to do it for you or
look at another option entirely. You may ask friends
and neighbors if anyone has a teenager that would be
willing to do the work for you for cheap or exchange
babysitting with a friend who is capable of doing the
work.

Check in your town for things such as free mulch. Our
town gives out free mulch twice a month. They can
dump a load in the back of a truck but you have to
shovel it out when you get home. We have done this
before. It took me, with some help from my husband
and a friend who stopped by, a week to shovel out the

back of the truck but we had more mulch than we needed and it cost us nothing but some exercise.

Don't be afraid to stop and ask! If you see a pile of paving stones, dirt, wood, or other materials in someone's yard or field, stop and ask if they need it hauled off.

Some states will allow you to pick up rocks along the side of public roads. Check the laws in your state. This is a great way to get large rocks that would cost a great deal if you bought them at a garden center or green house.

Remodeling

Remodeling is why all the home improvement stores stay in business. We are always trying to upgrade, update, or generally upscale our homes and property. If you aren't careful, remodeling won't pay off when you go to sell your home so it is important to look at each project individually. Are you doing it to make money when you sell, make your life easier or more aesthetic, or a mixture of both? Any option can be done frugally but if you are just trying to make money when you sell you may want to put some extra thought into what you are doing. For instance, there is only so much remodeling you can do when you live in a mobile home. Mobile homes have a higher saturation point than other homes; there comes a point when your home just won't make you anymore money as banks will not loan as much on a mobile home as they will a stick built.

Constant State of Remodel

I like to say that since day one of purchasing our own home and land we have been in a constant state of remodel. We began living in our single wide by placing our mattress on the floor of the kitchen and tearing through the house pulling up all of the flooring and ripping off the wallpaper as we went along. We then spent the next few years just keeping it livable, from the winter we spent a week without electric heat and huddled in the kitchen with the gas stove on, to the time we had to tear up the entire floor of our bedroom in the middle of a snow storm while water pipes and our hot water heater sprayed us down, to the month and a half we spent without air conditioning because we didn't want to fix the unit since we were getting a new one with the delivery of the double wide.

Our remodeling days were not over with the new home. The walls had to have the floral wall board painted over, new flooring put in, bathrooms gutted, decks built, and a garage addition. I guess not all those items had to be done. We could have lived with the pink and blue floral explosion throughout the house or the ancient vinyl that spread across the kitchen and dining room, but the rest was necessary and had to be done on a minimum of money. With help from family and friends and a great deal of hard labor, we got it all done and, even adding in the cost of remodeling, our home and land was still under half of what our friends owed on their homes.

Major Construction

Additions and any other construction aren't events that you can just decide to do on a Saturday afternoon. They take planning, help, and more often than not, some money, to complete.

Before beginning any kind of major construction call your city and county for any permits you need to get or rules you need to follow. You may not be able to do certain aspects yourself, such as electrical work, or you may need an inspector to come out periodically throughout the building process.

Supplies can be purchased on sale, through people who have bought excess and no longer need it on local classifieds or through word of mouth, or you can look for places such as Habitat for Humanity stores that sell excess supplies for much cheaper than you would find in a home improvement store.

Do the work yourself to save money and call in friends and family who are knowledgeable in construction to help. When we decided to double the size of our garage we asked my husband's parents to come down and help us build it. They stayed with us for a few months and my father-in-law and I built the garage with help from my mother-in-law, nephew, and my husband when he wasn't at work. We saved a bundle in not having to hire someone and we got to spend time with family. If this isn't possible you may want to see about exchanging services with someone who does know how to do the work you need. If you do have to hire a professional then make sure they are licensed and bonded and ask for referrals before you make a decision. The cheapest bid doesn't always equal the best work.

Paint and Flooring

While a lot of us may not be able to do major construction, most of us can paint a wall. Buying the cheapest paint and supplies is not often the most frugal option. Cheap paint may not cover well and you will find that you use double the amount to cover a stubborn wall when you may have needed half the amount of the more expensive brand. The same goes for paint supplies. A good brush will get you through many years if you take care of it and make sure to clean it well after each use while the cheap brushes fall apart.

Paint is also a great frugal decorating option. It allows you to change the look and feel of a room somewhat frequently without spending a great deal of money while creating a big impact.

Flooring is becoming more do-it-yourself as well. Not all flooring products are easy enough for the first time installer but many products, such as laminates, can be put down by amateurs. Look for close-outs at flooring stores and save money by installing it yourself.

Keep your floor clean so that it lasts longer and purchase a quality pad for under your carpet. A quality pad will help your carpet last longer than the cheapest pad will. Vacuuming and cleaning up spills will keep it looking good longer as well.

General Remodeling

You can find many of the supplies needed for general remodeling at the same places you would find supplies for major construction projects. You may also find items such as cabinets, toilets, or other smaller items at garage or estate sales.

Don't forget to let everyone know that you are remodeling your home. You may be surprised to find how much people have that they no longer need that they will just give you or will sell for cheap.

My parents recently remodeled their entire home and added on an addition. This project meant we were able to get their old bathroom vanity and a toilet for our master bath. We were able to remodel our master bathroom for the cost of a few plumbing supplies and we received quality products that we would not have been able to otherwise afford.

Check resale places as well, especially ReStore resale outlets through Habitat for Humanity, they get a great deal of construction materials donated to them so they are able to sell them for a fraction of what you would pay otherwise. You are also helping Habitat for Humanity so it is a win-win situation!

Chapter 14

Weddings

Marital bliss does not begin with going broke trying to get to the altar. A wedding does not have to cost in the tens of thousands to be beautiful, nor does it have to cost a bundle for the bride to feel like she had the best day of her life. Remember that people are there to celebrate your love and marriage, not how much money you can spend in one day.

Going to the Chapel

We didn't actually go to a chapel to get married, as we got married outside, but our wedding helped me come up with a great deal of frugal ideas for a wedding, either because my mom came up with great ideas to cut costs or because afterwards we realized where we could have saved money. Our wedding was stunning, it didn't cost tens of thousands of dollars, and not one person stated to us that they would have liked it more if we had just spent some more money.

I had never been the kind of girl who spent a great deal of time thinking about her wedding. I had never looked through a wedding or bridal magazine and I had managed up to that point to have only been in one wedding. I didn't really know what to expect, nor did I know what was, or wasn't, possible. The best thing you can do before your wedding is research. What would you like to have? Design your dream wedding and then pair it down so that if fits within your budget.

The Budget

Create a Wedding Budget just like you would for your own finances or a vacation. Stick to it as much as you can but also allow for it to vary as estimates from vendors come in or decide what you can do without if you have to cut some thing. Decide what is most important to you, perhaps the dress or the location, and make sure that you budget for it while realizing that you may have to take away from another area such as the cake or a DJ.

Bridesmaids and Groomsmen

The easiest way, of course, to not have to worry about the monetary aspect of bridesmaids and groomsmen is to just not have them but this isn't always practical as for some, there just wouldn't be a wedding without them. If you do have them make sure you think through whom you want to say that you had in your wedding twenty years after the decorations have been put away.

Ask your bridesmaids and groomsmen to purchase, or rent, their own apparel but do not choose gowns or suits that will cause them to go broke as well. You could shop for bridesmaid dresses during prom season at non-wedding stores. My bridesmaid dresses were beautiful dresses that we found at a teen store in the mall. They were actually prom dresses that we got for less than $50 each. My sister even got to reuse hers by wearing it to her prom and in another wedding.

It is expected that gifts are given to the bridesmaids and groomsmen for taking the time to be involved in your big day. You don't have to go all out on the gifts, simple is just as good and just as appreciated. Look for costume jewelry to wear that day or a nice compact for the girls and money clips or pocket knives for the guys.

Deciding on a Wedding Time and Date

You can save a great deal of money just by changing the time of your wedding. You could have an early morning wedding and serve a simple brunch afterwards or you can have an afternoon wedding and serve hors d'oeuvres instead of a full dinner. Also, these times generally mean there is no alcohol served and a reception can be small and intimate or you could skip the reception entirely.

Look at having your wedding during the off-season, November to April, but try to stay away from the holidays like Christmas or Valentine's Day. Since weddings usually happen May to October you have a better chance of getting a deal through the vendors in your area during the off season.

Invitations

With all of the technology most of us have in our homes there is no reason not to make your own invitations. Both my sister and I got a lot of compliments on our invitations and they were printed right off my mom's printer! Not only does this save you money but you can personalize it any way you want so that your invitations are unique to you.

If you do purchase invitations go for a simple look without a great deal of inserts to save money. Remember that most people are just going to throw it away which means you are just throwing money away if you make it too fancy!

Ceremony and Reception

When deciding on where to have your ceremony and reception you may want to consider an outdoor or backyard wedding. These places may not only cost less (or free!) but you can often combine the ceremony and the reception in one spot instead of having to rent two venues.

Outdoor weddings also mean that you can spend less on decorations as the environment makes for a great backdrop. Keeping it simple doesn't just mean a more inexpensive wedding but it will also mean less stress as the big day approaches.

If you do choose to have your ceremony or reception in a building then remember that a few white (not multi-colored!) holiday lights and turning down the main lights can make even the simplest of décor look rich and inviting.

Flowers

Flowers for your wedding can break the budget if you aren't careful. Go with simple arrangements and choose flowers that are in season in order to get the most flowers for your budget.

Arrange your flowers yourself to save money. Even better, grab a family member or friend with a green thumb and have them grow the flowers for your wedding.

Food and Cake

The food and the cake are big budget busters as well but you can easily cut back on money without cutting back on style. While it is often expected that you will feed the guests who took the time to come to your wedding, no where is it stated that you have to feed them lobster and filet mignon. A simple pasta and salad makes a nice presentation and will not cost much.

If you are having a backyard wedding then think about having a potluck. You don't have to necessarily ask everyone to bring a dish but you may have several friends and family who would be glad to help cook a large dish to bring.

The cake is often most important for pictures but it isn't always even eaten. Consider cupcakes instead of a cake. They look just as elegant when placed on a cupcake tier and will be much cheaper instead of a large, fancy cake that ends up in the trash. Guests are also more likely to go up and take a cupcake than a piece of cake. Cupcakes can also be frozen which means the cost for making them can be spread out (buy a box a week until they are all made), as well as making sure they are done before the wedding day.

If cupcakes just aren't your thing, have one small fancy cake made to cut for pictures with the bride and groom and have a plain white sheet cake made for the guests.

Centerpieces

Centerpieces liven up the reception hall and create an inviting space for your guests to sit down in. A great centerpiece is to use the cupcakes. This gives everyone their own personal cupcake, and will mean there is less waste, as few will be able to pass it up when it is right in front of them!

Float flowers in bowls of water. Shop around for sales on glass bowls before the wedding or borrow from family or friends. Bowls or vases could also be filled with seeds, peas, even sticks! If the bride and groom have a sweet tooth, fill the bowls with their favorite candy, especially if it is colorful.

Make the centerpieces yourself instead of hiring people to make them. This will save you a great deal and will let you spend some quality time before the wedding putting them together with friends and family.

Entertainment

Weddings aren't usually just fun on their own and the entertainment can make or break a reception. Hire a DJ over a band for a better price, unless you personally know a band that will give you a great deal. If this is still too much then rent a sound system that will hook to your MP3 player and play whatever you want.

Alcohol is an expensive aspect to the entertainment. Go with no alcohol if you do not approve or if the budget or venue does not allow. If you want it but just can't have an open bar then make it a cash bar or BYOB, just make sure to note it on the invitation.

Favors

Favors can get expensive when you are trying to send each person who attends home with one, so think outside the box. Make the favors yourself by wrapping candy or having a candy buffet with bags the guests themselves can fill. Seed packets with the bride and grooms favorite flowers are also a great idea.

Gifts

The registry is important and is there for a reason. Often the registry will hold what the bride and groom most need, especially as many brides and grooms are older and may already have a blender nor do many purchase things like crystal any more. If you are the bride and groom and have no need for extra things then think about a honeymoon registry where others can contribute to your honeymoon or have people give to your favorite charity.

When you are the one attending the wedding as a guest you can give frugal gifts that won't go to waste (or end up in the next garage sale), especially if you decide to purchase something off the registry. Depending on your intimacy with the couple, a scrapbook or photobook of the pictures you have of them, nice journals, a family recipe book, a tool set (for him and her!), a board game gift basket, or a gift card for a movie and popcorn. Two of my favorite gift ideas (works for housewarming gifts as well!) are holiday decor (make sure you buy on sale right after the holidays!) or a laundry basket full of cleaning supplies.

Chapter 15

Moving On Up

Moving from one home to another is one of the top stresses in life. It can also be one of the most expensive. Finding ways to save money in what is often a very expensive process can be a difficult thing to do though you can move on a budget!

10 Moves, 10 Chances to Get It Right

We have moved ten times in the 16 years we have been together, and are getting ready to do it one more time as we move into our new house. Most of our early moves were haphazard events in which we were just trying to get from one spot to the other and did not even consider things like a budget. There were times we would move into a house and not even have the money to get the electric turned on for a few days. Thank goodness, those times did not last long!

We did get better at it and it is a much easier process now. We planned out our last two moves and are in the planning stages of our next one. It was a much easier process when planned and we don't have to worry about if the electric will get turned on or not as the money for the deposit (if we even have to pay one due to our excellent credit) is already put aside.

Practice makes perfect and we have definitely had practice at moving!

Packing

Packing is one of my favorite parts of moving. I love that I get to go through everything and get rid of what we no longer need. Packing isn't about throwing everything you own into a trash bag and hoping for the best (though we have done that in our pre-frugal incarnation).

This is your chance to go through every item you own. Create a pile for donations, one for trash, and pack up what is left. Make sure that you pack like things with like and clearly label the boxes. The boxes should state what is inside of them as well as what room they go in at the new home. This makes for much easier unpacking.

Look for free boxes at stores or on online classified sites like Craigslist. Often people will get rid of boxes after they have moved. If you have friends or family who are moving before you are ask them to save their boxes for you.

We have used free boxes before but this last time we purchased most of our moving boxes. I purchased both cardboard and plastic storage. The plastic storage will be used once we get moved in to store my holiday décor, fabric and my husband's tools and garage stuff that he needs organized. All of these items are currently stored in old cardboard copy paper boxes that are falling apart. I knew we could get one more move out of them but then they needed to be stored in new bins and boxes. If you do find that you need to buy moving boxes you may want to think about how you can use it afterwards.

Budget Moving Expenses

There are so many ways you can spend money when moving that having a budget and money already saved up is a must. Think about things such as paying people to help you move if you do not have friends or family nearby to help, gas back and forth from your old home to your new, feeding you and anyone who is helping you, and deposits, whether for renting or turning on utilities.

We were surprised at how much gas we needed to move and wish we had budgeted a bit more. We had to take several more trips than we anticipated and filling up our truck each time was hard on the checking account.

Eating out was another area we spent quite a bit of money on. Several weeks before the move in which we sold our home, I prepared and froze meals to heat up while we were moving so that we didn't have to eat out. I also purchased some convenience foods that I would not normally purchase, such as single serve microwave rice, pre-cooked chicken, and frozen dinners. While these meals were used we also ate out a great deal. There were nights after moving for ten hours that the thought of a frozen dinner was more than we could stand. The stress was overwhelming and we just wanted some French fries. We ended up wanting a lot of French fries and, healthy or not, that was what we needed at that time. It just made the process easier on us at the time.

Buying and Selling a Home

Buying and selling our homes took more money than we expected. There were unexpected expenses and expenses that we didn't realize were a part of buying and selling because we hadn't gone through the full process before, at least not on this scale.

A storage unit or interim housing may be in your moving future as well. We were lucky enough that a duplex was available for us to live in during the two months between selling our previous home and purchasing our new one. While this gave us a place to stay, it would not hold all of our things. We had to rent a storage unit and a post office box. Realize that you may have to rent a place while moving or a storage unit until you can fully move into your new home.

When you put your home up for sale you have several things you will have to spend money on.

  Staging – This doesn't have to cost much, or anything, but you do need to stage your home for sale. Remove all of your clutter and personal items such as family pictures. Set your house up like a show home.

If necessary, repaint the walls a neutral color. We only spent $50 to stage our home. I purchased new towels and rugs from Dollar General for both the bathroom and the kitchen. They added a pop of color and looked better than our old and worn out towels and rugs. I also purchased some new plants with blooming flowers to add some color to our living room.

Fixing Broken Items – Fix the things that you can see our wrong with your home. Fixing trim, leaky faucets and doors that stick will make people look at your home better. Most don't want a home they will have to do a great deal of work on. We fixed a leak in our roof, a leaky faucet, and we had replaced the vinyl in our entry way.

Inspections – Be prepared to fix things that will come up in the inspections, and things will come up. Even brand new houses can have problems. We had several issues as well as termites in our garage. We treated the termites, which took a large chunk of money, and negotiated the sale price for the rest of the issues. While the only money we were out at this time was the termite treatment we also had to take away some of our profit on the house sale in order to keep the sale going forward. Don't start spending your profit until the day of closing when you put that check in your pocket.

Gas and food – We had to leave each time our home was shown to potential buyers. This meant a great deal of gas to come and go from the house as we had a lot of showings. We also ate out some during this time as showings would often land during dinner time.

Buying a home costs as well, and not just the down payment.

Down Payment – It is best if you have a sizeable down payment for your home though, if your credit is excellent and you live in certain areas, there are still 100% financing options available.

Inspections – This time you are the one paying for the inspections. We spent almost $600 to have our home and lagoon inspected and a termite inspection. Our home also has a fireplace which would normally need to be inspected as well but we decided to have it cleaned and inspected in the fall. Also, if an inspection comes back and informs you that the house has too many problems, you still have to pay for the inspection even if you are not purchasing the house. You would then have to have the money for the next wave of inspections at a new home.

Gas – It costs a great deal to drive around looking at houses, especially if they are not in the same area as the house you are selling.

Interim Housing – Be prepared in case you sell your home and haven't yet purchased a new one, which is what we did! We had almost two months between leaving one house before getting in the next. We had to have housing, utilities, and internet for that time, as well as a storage unit to hold our things.

Home ownership is an expensive process but we are very glad we have done it.

Chapter 16

The End

Living a frugal lifestyle isn't about being cheap or a miser. It is about getting the best value for your money. You can be frugal in any income range. Frugal living is also much like a diet, if you fall off the wagon just get right back on!

A frugal life doesn't mean never doing something spontaneous or extravagant but it is about being in such a financially responsible spot that those kinds of splurges do not mean you spend weeks wondering if your electric is going to get shut off or how you are going to make your house payment.

Include your entire family, make a plan, and have fun on your frugal journey!

Printed in Great Britain
by Amazon

78597034R00059